197426

UP CLOSE™

MICRO BUGS

PAUL HARRISON

PowerKiDS
press.

New York

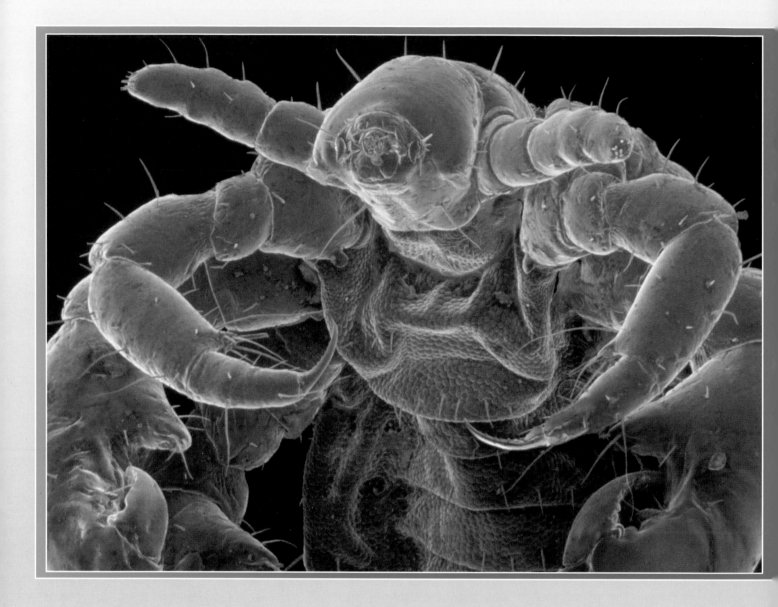

Published in 2007 by The Rosen Publishing Group, Inc.
29 East 21st Street, New York, NY 10010

Copyright © 2007 Arcturus Publishing Limited

Author: Paul Harrison
Editor (new edition): Ella Fern
Designers (new edition): Steve West, Steve Flight

Picture credits: NHPA: 8 bottom; Science Photo Library: front and back
cover, title page, 2, 4, 5 top, middle, bottom, 6, 7 top, bottom, 8 top,
9, 10 top, bottom, 11, 12, 13 top, bottom, 14, 15 top, bottom, 16, 17,
18, 19 top, middle, 20, 21 top, middle.

Library of Congress Cataloging-in-Publication Data

Harrison, Paul, 1969-
 Micro bugs / Paul Harrison.
   p. cm. -- (Up close)
 Includes index.
 ISBN-13: 978-1-4042-3760-5 (library binding)
 ISBN-10: 1-4042-3760-7 (library binding)
 1. Parasites--Juvenile literature. 2. Arthropod pests--Juvenile
literature. 3. Microorganisms--Juvenile literature. I. Title.
 QL757.H32 2007
 578.6'5--dc22

                      2006033001

Manufactured in China

Contents

What Are Micro Bugs?

We see animals all around us every single day, whether they're birds sitting on telephone wires, cows in fields, or pets curled up at home. But did you know there are millions of other animals out there that you can only really see properly under a microscope? They're rummaging around on your clothes, living on your furniture and right this minute they're probably crawling on you! Feeling itchy yet?

The first person to look at micro bugs was the Dutchman Antony van Leeuwenhoek during the 1670s—he also invented the forerunner of the modern microscope.

MITES

The biggest family of microscopic animals is the mites and, with over 30,000 different species, each mite has a lot of cousins! Most mites are less than 0.04 inches (1 mm) in length and can be found practically everywhere on earth—from hot deserts to cold deserts, on top of mountains and below the sea. All mites are part of the arthropod family, which makes them distant relatives of spiders.

BUGS

Of course, not all the microscopic marvels that you'll find in this book are mites. There are a whole variety of other bugs that only really come to light using a microscope. Insects are one of the largest animal groups on earth, so it's not surprising that some of them are really tiny—there are so many species that they're bound to come in all shapes and sizes, aren't they?

ELECTRON MICROSCOPE

The study of micro bugs really took off with the invention of the electron microscope in 1931 by Ernst Ruska, for which he was awarded the Nobel Prize in 1986. The beauty of these microscopes is that they use electrons instead of light to view specimens, and can magnify an object much more than a traditional microscope, giving us the ability to view these tiny creatures very closely indeed.

NEMATODES

Nematodes are like small worms—so small that many of them can only be seen under a microscope. Scientists aren't sure how many different sorts of nematodes there are as they believe only a small percentage of the different varieties have been discovered so far. Although nematodes are quite simple creatures, some of them have a neat trick. When it gets too hot or too cold they can go into a kind of suspended animation until the climate improves.

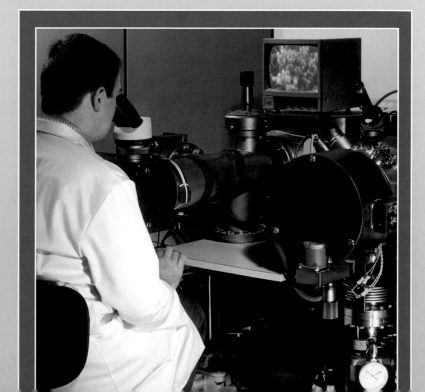

n the past, houses used to be riddled with microscopic lodgers looking for somewhere cozy to live. Thankfully, things change, and improved levels of hygiene mean that these uninvited guests aren't as numerous as before. But no matter how clean your house is, there will still be mites lurking somewhere.

BED AND BREAKFAST

Are you aware that you might be sharing your bed at night? And we're not just talking about one other body here—we're talking about thousands of tiny bed-sharers! One mattress-loving little monster is the bed bug. These flat-bodied, reddish-brown creatures used to be very common in the past and are making something of a comeback. They love to hide in mattresses and feed on people's blood at night.

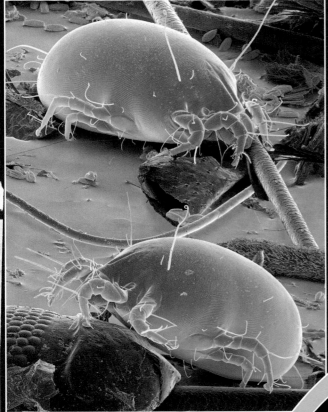

Thankfully, most beds don't have bed bugs, but they do have dust mites. These mites live all around the house, though most of them are found in beds. This is because beds are full of tiny bits of people's skin flakes—and this is what dust mites eat. In fact, beds are such good sources of food that mattresses can be home to tens of thousands of these little critters.
If that thought isn't bad enough, just remember all these mites poop as well—and guess where they do it? Yep, in your bed.

MITEY CLIMB

This dust mite has made it up to the top of a needle—which should give you an idea of how big—or small—it is. Because there are so many dust mites around, they cause problems even when they die. Their decaying bodies are thought to cause allergic reactions in humans. No wonder!

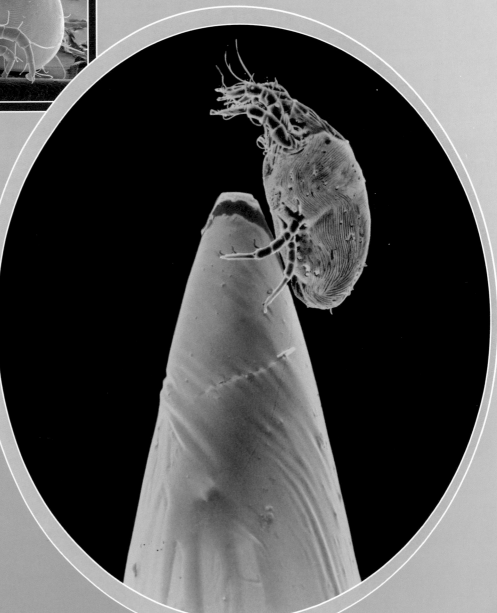

FOOD FOR FRIENDS

The news that food mites are as partial to your favorite snacks as you are will probably ruin your appetite, but it's true. These food mites are often very pale in color, measure less than 0.02 inches (0.5 mm) long and can be found on cheese, flour, sugar and cereals, among a number of other foods. What's more, if you eat them—which would be easy to do as they're so small—they could make you feel a bit queasy (if you're not already).

LIFE IN THE LIBRARY

Although they are called book lice, in truth these leg lice will eat a whole range of foods, just like food mit do. They love warm and humid environments, and houses and libraries are the perfect places for them, remember to be careful with your books—especially this one!

When people see bits of paper dust flying about they sometimes think they're looking at paper mites but actually there's no such thing.

Personal Parasites

With so many tiny bugs and mites out there it's not really surprising that some of them call humans home. You might not want to think about it, but your body is just the place where a whole host of micro monsters want to settle down and raise a family.

HAIR RAISING

One tiny pest which you're more likely to meet than most is the head louse, or nit. At around 0.08 inches (2 mm) long they are smaller than their close relation, the body louse, but that doesn't mean they aren't annoying. Their saliva irritates the skin making the head itch. What's more they leave lots of eggs attached to your hair. Nits actually prefer clean hair, but that's no excuse for not washing it!

LOUSY BODY

The body louse—the big brother of the head louse—lives on people's bodies and clothes. It doesn't like cleanliness as much as its small relation, so having a bath's a good idea. However, unlike head lice who die soon after being separated from their hairy home, body lice can survive for days waiting for a new body to come along.

EYE EYE

Believe it or not, there's even a type of mite that lives on your eyelashes! It's called the follicle mite because it lives in your follicles, the pits in your skin where the roots of your hairs are, in particular those on your face. It likes to feed on the oily secretions from your skin.

UP CLOSE

This follicle mite has come out to play. Even though they live close to your eyes, you'd have trouble seeing them, —they're less than 0.02 inches (0.5 mm) long!

ITCHY AND SCRATCHY

Little mites can sometimes cause big problems. Chiggers like this one, which are actually baby red mites, sometimes bite adults leaving sore, itchy welts. More seriously, the scabies mite can burrow into your skin, leaving wounds which get covered in hard, itchy scabs. These can become infected if scratched too hard.

There is a type of itch mite that normally feeds on pine oak leaves, but if these are in short supply they will happily nibble on people instead —leaving sore, red bite marks.

Animal Antics

If you think that we humans can suffer from the mischief that micro bugs can cause, then spare a thought for other animals. They get attacked by a much bigger range of tiny terrors than we do and the results can be a lot more painful.

JUMP TO IT

One pet parasite you may have encountered before on a dog or cat is the flea. Under an electron microscope you can really see what these jumpy little guys look like. Adult fleas emerge from pupae (a kind of cocoon), but if no food is available these young adults can stay in their snug little homes for months waiting for lunch to pass by. Fleas can feel vibrations and even the heat given off by people and animals. When they get the signal, they can start munching.

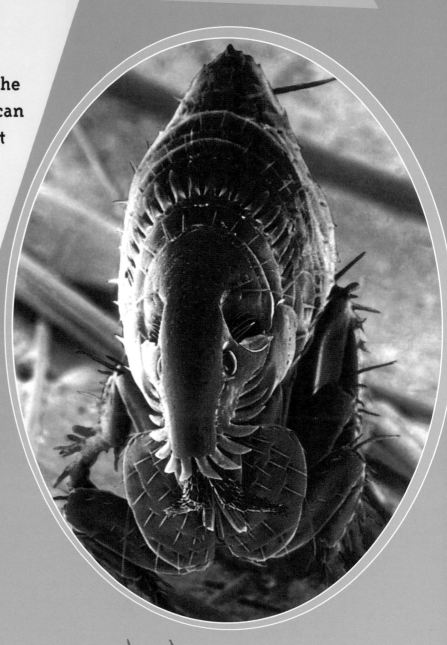

There is even one type of mite which likes to live on cats' ears!

BEE MITE

FOWL MITE

Like most birds, chickens can be infested with mites. In the chicken's case the mite in question is often called the fowl mite. It sucks the bird's blood causing irritation and a possible reduction in the number of eggs the bird can lay. And guess where these mites like to live? Around chickens' bottoms! Yuck!

You wouldn't think an animal as small as a bee would have other tiny insects using it as a free lunch, but it's true! Bees suffer from the attentions of the varroa mite and the tracheal mite. The varroa mite and the tracheal mite are both potentially fatal to the poor infected bee. The varroa mite, like the one pictured, sucks the blood of both adult and young bees while the tracheal mite lives in the bees' breathing tubes.

MANGY MUTT

Animals suffer from scabies just like humans do. Often it is referred to as mange and it can cause itchiness, hair loss and the unfortunate animal can also lose weight. Actually there are different types of mange—sheep can suffer from one caused by the foot scab mite which only attacks the skin above the foot.

13

Plant Pests

Well, your house is covered in mites, your pet is covered in bugs and you're probably crawling with them yourself, but if you think the garden will be a place of refuge from these microscopic mischief-makers then think again. The outside is teeming with the little pests!

EATS SHOOTS AND LEAVES

Nematodes can be a particular problem for plants—especially as the soil is chock-full of these wormy marvels. Shoot nematodes live inside plant leaves and can cause them to lose color or die. Other types of nematodes attack the roots of plants which can affect how the plant develops. They can slow down how quickly a plant grows, or even trick the plant into growing the bits which the nematodes like to eat. Now how cool is that?

GALLING

Have you ever seen a plant with odd looking lumps and bumps that don't seem to belong to it? They're called galls and can be caused by a variety of means; but it will come as no surprise to learn that micro bugs are one of the major reasons behind these disfigurements. Some galls can even form on the roots of plants, which can be the result of hungry nematodes underground. Galls start out looking fleshy—like this one—and become hard and woody as they get older.

FOOD FOR LIFE

Some galls, such as bud galls and velvet galls, are formed by mites feeding. Up to eight generations of mites are born each year, and most spend their whole lives inside the gall. Sometimes the mites abandon the gall, so it drops off and the plant returns to the way it was before.

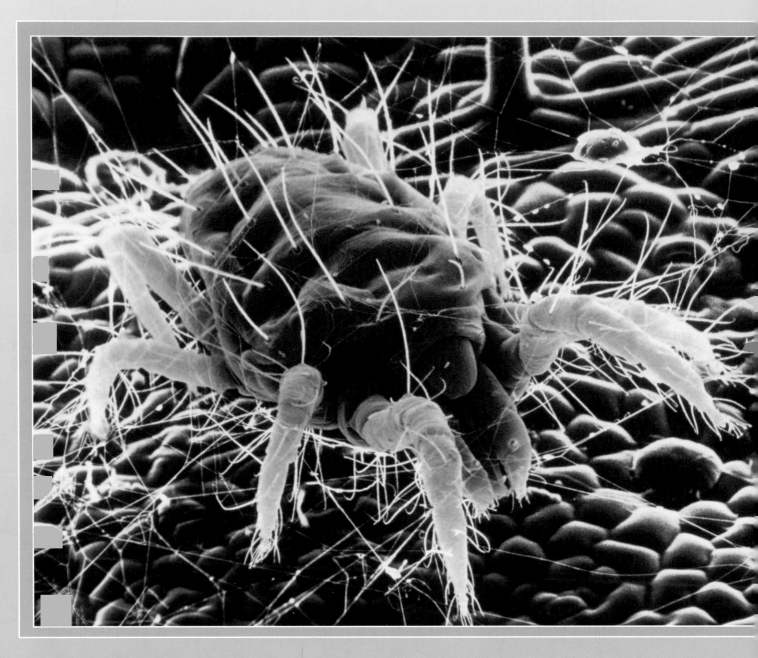

A MITEY PROBLEM

Gardeners hate red spider mites because these particular pests can turn up in both the garden and the greenhouse—and they like to eat just about all the things you do, such as strawberries and peas for example.

The red spider mite isn't really a spider at all – and is only really red in color during the autumn and winter.

SPRING BREAK

Some mites, such as the clover mite, like nothing more than the taste of fresh young seedlings. In the clover mites' case they drink the sap of grass and, no prizes for guessing it, clover too. These odd-looking mites have two very long front legs and can be found in large numbers in early spring.

Tiniest of All

A lthough some ticks and lice are so small you need a microscope to see them, they're not the smallest residents of our micro bug world; that award goes to the microbes. Microbes can be found everywhere and there are so many of them in the world your head would explode just thinking about it. There are lots of different types of microbes, but the main groups are: bacteria, protozoa, fungi, algae and viruses.

MOVERS AND SHAKERS

Protozoa are the microbes on the move. Some get about by beating a long thin tail, like a tadpole; others have lots of small hair-like bits sticking out over their bodies which they beat to shift themselves along. Protozoa move about to try to find food—and in some cases this means bacteria.

JUST ROTTEN

You've seen a member of the fungus family before if you've ever seen a mushroom; but some of its relatives are much smaller than that. Two of the most common are molds and yeast, which you need to bake bread. Algae, on the other hand, can be seen on top of still water (not the type you drink out of a bottle!)—it's the green scummy-looking stuff.

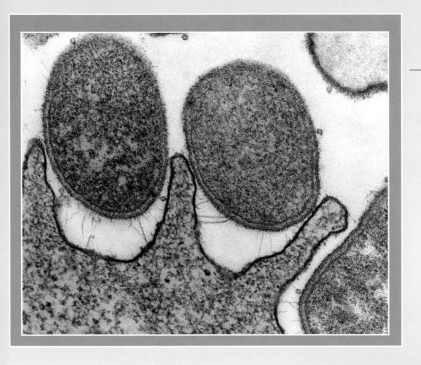

BACTERIA

Of all the microbes the most numerous are the bacteria. They can be found in water, in the soil and on animals and people. Bacteria come in all sorts of shapes and sizes and live in some of the most inhospitable places on earth, like deep sea vents, where seawater has seeped down deep into the earth's crust through cracks and fissures in the ocean floor, and in swamp mud. What a nice place to call home!

DEAD OR ALIVE

One controversial member of the microbe clan is the virus. There is some debate as to whether viruses can be classified as living things or not. What is not in doubt is what viruses can do. Most of the time viruses—like the flu virus—don't do anything, but sit there, or float around in the air. But if they come into contact with a person (or even an animal or plant) they immediately get busy reproducing and making the unlucky host feel distinctly unwell.

Microbes are the oldest living things on the planet. Scientists have found fossils of microbes dating back around 3.5 million years.

Good Buy, Bad Buy

So far, we've seen — quite literally in some cases — what a pain micro bugs can be. However, this is not always the case — sometimes these tiny critters can be very useful. Though that's not to say that some of them can't be bad for your health.

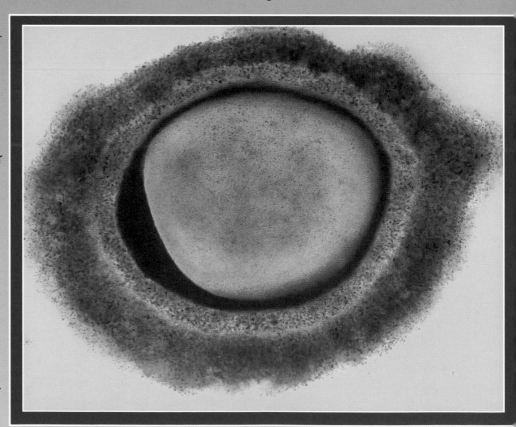

There is even a type of microbe which lives inside termites' stomachs. The Trichonympha flagellate helps the termite to digest the wood it eats.

NOT-SO-SUPER

One of the scariest types of microbes are the so called super bugs. These are bacteria which seem to be able to resist doctors' attempts to kill them off with antibiotics. The most famous super bugs are MRSA and E-coli. They have been responsible for a number of deaths after patients contracted the bacteria—in hospitals of all places! This is because super bugs only affect people who are ill and whose resistance has been weakened. Healthy people aren't affected at all—in fact some scientists believe that over 10% of people carry super bugs on their skin with no ill effects.

GARDEN FRIEND OR FOE

We've already discovered that nematodes can be bad news for plants; but that's not always the case. Some are so useful at eating other problem insects that gardeners actually buy them. The Steinernema and Heterorhabditis families of nematodes are two particular favorites for controlling a whole range of uninvited garden pests.

COUGHS AND SNEEZES

Bacteria and viruses are well known for the bad things they do—like giving us a bout of flu or a cold—but bacteria can be really useful, too. And on a large scale. One of the biggest dangers to life living by the coast is the damage an oil spill out at sea can wreak. Now scientists have discovered there are some types of bacteria which will eat some of the elements which make up gas and oil, and these bacteria can be used to help reduce the impact of the oil spills.

GUT FEELING

Remember the microbes? Well, one of the really useful things they do is help us to digest our food. You may not like the thought of microbes living inside your gut, but without them that lump of soggy, chewed up pizza you've just swallowed would stay like a lump of soggy, chewed up pizza for a lot longer. Each person has over 10 trillion microbes in his or her body.

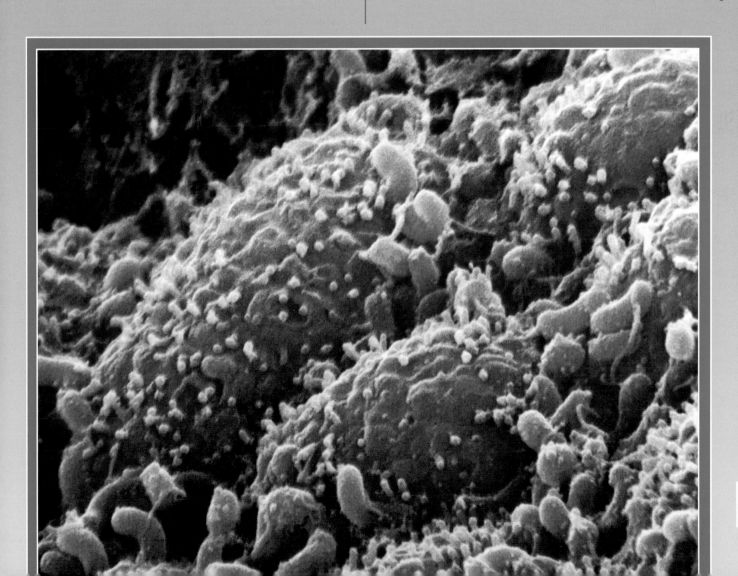

Glossary

Algae (AL-jee)
Organisms that live in water, ranging in size from single cells to large weeds.

Arthropod (AHR-thruh-pahd)
An invertebrate with a segmented body and an exoskeleton (skeleton outside the body). Arthropods include crustaceans, insects and arachnids (spiders).

Bacteria (bak-TIR-ee-uh)
Microscopic cells that can cause disease, but also help with processes such as digestion and decomposition.

Cocoon (keh-KOON)
A protective covering often made of silk that covers an insect during its transformation into an adult.

Ernst Ruska (1906-1988) (URNST ROO-skuh)
The scientist who invented the electron microscope in 1933.

Flea (FLEE)
A minute blood-sucking parasite that lives on the skin of animals and birds.

Follicles (FOH-lih-kulz)
Small cavities on the body that contain or protect each hair.

Fungi (FUN-jy)
Like bacteria, fungi are organisms that help to break down organic matter.

Gall (GOL)
Abnormal growth on a tree or plant caused by some insects, bacteria or fungi.

Humid (HYOO-med)
Warm and moist.

Hygiene (HY-jeen)
Keeping clean and sanitary.

Infested (in-FEST-ed)
When a human or animal is covered in mites or lice.

Louse (plural: lice) (LAUS)
A tiny blood-sucking parasite.

Mange (MAYNJ)
A skin infection caused by mites that causes hair loss. Mange mostly affects domestic animals.

Microbe (MY-krohb)
A microscopic organism, usually a germ.

Microscopic (my-kreh-SKAH-pik)
Something that is not visible to the naked eye, and must be looked at using a microscope.

Mite (MYT)
A tiny blood-sucking parasite from the arachnid (spider) family.

Nematode (NEE-muh-tohd)
A tiny worm-like bug that lives outside.

Nit (NIT)
A head louse that lays eggs in people's hair.

Parasite (PER-uh-syt)
A bug (or other animal or plant) that lives on another animal or plant and feeds off it.

Protozoa (proh-teh-ZOH-eh)
A type of microbe.

Pupa (plural: pupae) (PYOO-puh)
An insect that is transforming from a larva to an adult.

Scabies (SKAY-beez)
A contagious skin infection caused by mites.

Secretion (sih-KREE-shen)
A substance (usually oily) released from the skin.

Super bug (SOO-pur BUG)
A bug like E-coli or MRSA that cannot be killed by antibiotics.

Suspended animation (suh-SPEND-ed a-nuh-MAY-shun)
When something doesn't move at all, usually to save energy.

Virus (VY-rus)
A type of protein not even visible under a microscope that can replicate and cause disease.

Further Reading

The Best Book of Bugs
Claire Llewellyn, Kingfisher, 2005

The Big Book of Bugs
Theresa Greenaway, Dorling Kindersley, 2002

Bugs and Minibeasts
John Farndon, Southwater Books, 2002

Bug Hunters
Barbara Taylor, Chrysalis Children's Books, 2003

WEB SITES

Due to the changing nature of Internet links, PowerKids Press has developed an online list of Web sites related to this book. This site is updated regularly. Please use this link to access the list:
www.powerkidslinks.com/CCR/bugs/

Index